Maze Quest

ILLUSTRATED BY
LAURA HORTON
STORY BY
WILLIAM POTTER

ARCTURUS

HOW TO USE THIS BOOK

Most mazes in this book have more than one exit. When you reach the edge of a page, follow the instructions, turning to the page number indicated.

Sometimes your path will be blocked by obstacles or enemies. Go back and find a new route!

The start point to a maze is always indicated by Jada and Tim.

CRYSTAL FOREST

Cobble leads Jada and Tim into a sparkling forest, where crystalline creatures gambol among giant gems. See what you can find on your path through the glittering trees.

Wow! That huge shield fit into this magic pouch.

Watch where you step! Everything is made of crystal here, even the animals!

Collect the Sun Gem.

To the Valley of Wisps (page 10)

CAN YOU FIND ...

2   3   3

To the Shifting Swamp (page 6)

If you have the Eternal Flame, turn to page 12.

You will need to collect certain items by passing over them. You can make a record of the items you have collected in the checklist on page 3.

To complete the story, you must travel from page to page until you reach Amaza's Palace. You will need every item on the checklist to defeat her!

Some routes and exits are blocked unless you have the right item listed under your treasures. You may have to pass through some mazes twice to finish the book.

INTO THE MAZE

When Jada told her friend Tim she wanted to explore the Forgotten Forest, he pulled a face. "I'm just getting to a good bit in my adventure story!" Little did they realize that their walk in the woods would be the beginning of an incredible quest ...

This is so strange! Why would there be a door in a tree? Maybe we should leave it alone, in case someone lives inside?

No way! This has to be the start of an adventure. I'm definitely going in, and you're coming with me!

Pinned to the tree next to the door is a piece of parchment that looks like a checklist. What can it be for?

○ Winged Helmet
○ Singing Sword
○ Eagle-Eye Bow
○ Golden Gauntlet
○ Sea Queen's Trident
○ Climbing Gear
○ Chainmail Shirt

○ Invisibility Cloak
○ Sun Gem
○ Quest Clothes
○ River Raft
○ Eternal Flame
○ Ancient Shield
○ Diving Helmets

To the Crystal Forest (page 8)

Collect the Ancient Shield

CAN YOU FIND ...

3   1   6

7

Collect the Sun Gem.

To the Valley of Wisps (page 10)

CAN YOU FIND ...

2   3   3

If you have the Eternal Flame, turn to page 12.

VALLEY OF WISPS

Next, the trio arrive in a crumbling, forgotten town patrolled by ghostly creatures made of memories. Lead them through the maze and listen to Sage, the wise old wizard.

To the Shifting
Swamp (page 6)

Collect the Eternal Flame.

CAN YOU FIND ...

| 4 | 4 | 7 |

To the Crystal
Forest (page 8)

THE BURROWS

Jada, Tim, and Cobble descend into a twisting, turning labyrinth of underground tunnels. Jada holds the Eternal Flame high above her head, lighting the way.

Do you hear that drilling sound? There are borebeasts about!

CAN YOU FIND ...

1

3

7

To the Crystal Forest (page 8)

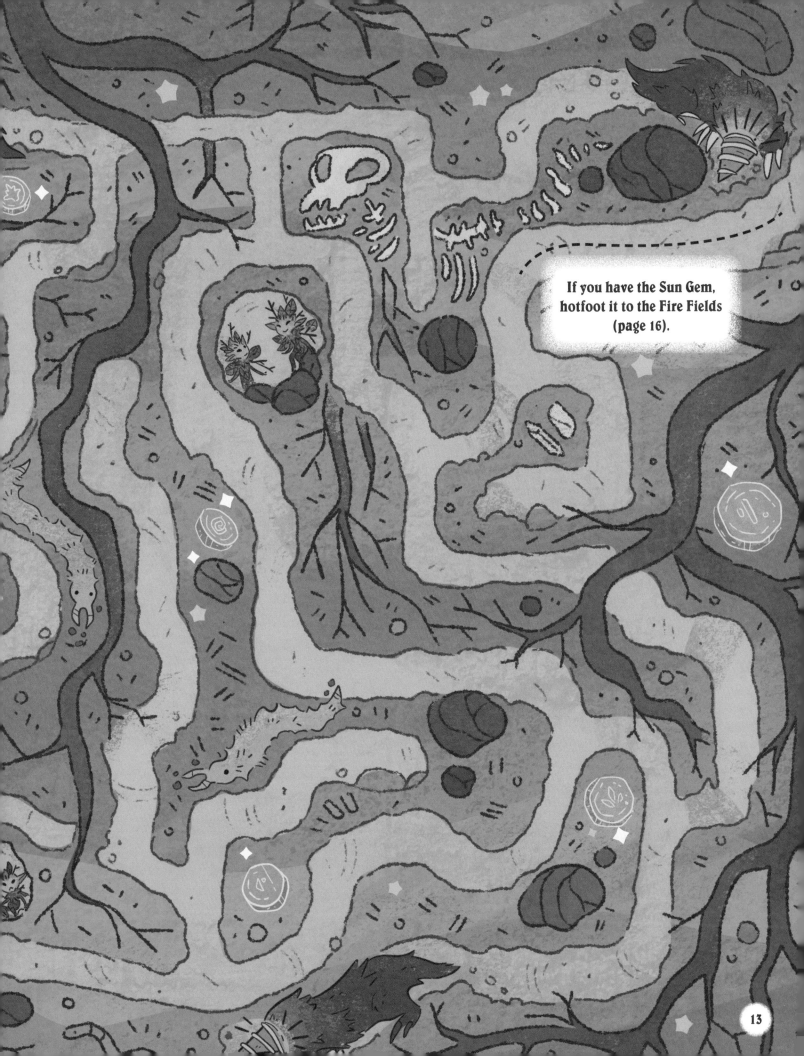

If you have the Sun Gem,
hotfoot it to the Fire Fields
(page 16).

LIGHTNING LAND

Look out! These lightning-wielding lords and ladies are clashing over ancient treasures. Dash through the danger zone!

Collect the Singing Sword.

Careful not to be hit by lightning!

How do we do that?

By being lucky!

CAN YOU FIND ...

3

5

7

To the Fire Fields
(page 16)

To the Burrows
(page 12)

To the Sparkling City (page 30)

To Bounceberg (page 28)

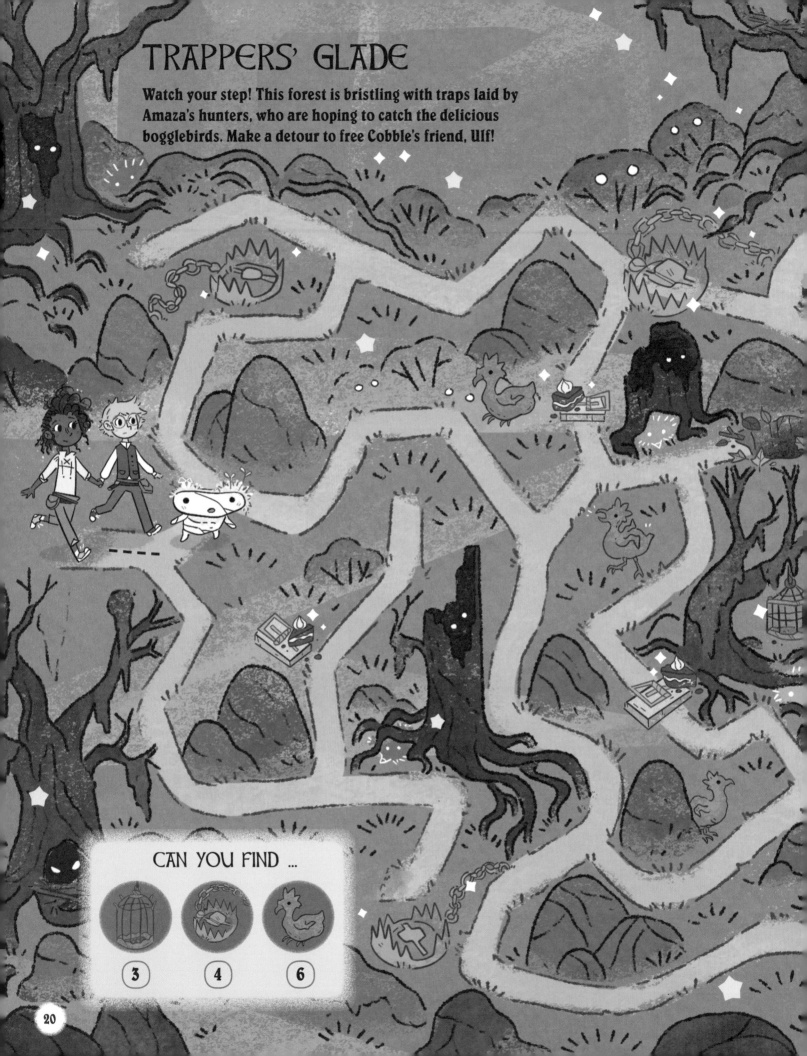

TRAPPERS' GLADE

Watch your step! This forest is bristling with traps laid by Amaza's hunters, who are hoping to catch the delicious bogglebirds. Make a detour to free Cobble's friend, Ulf!

CAN YOU FIND ...

3   4   6

If you have the
Climbing Gear,
clamber to page 22.

Collect the Climbing Gear.

To the Fire Fields
(page 16)

Untangle me from
this rope and I'll
help show you a
way out.

TOWER TREE

The rope and climbing gear the friends collected comes in handy right away—the next path is up a giant tree. Can you trace it?

To the Eyrie
(page 24)

CAN YOU FIND ...

3 4 5

To Trappers' Glade (page 20)

CAN YOU FIND ...

1 4 7

To the Sky
Kingdom
(page 26)

Collect the Chainmail Shirt

SKY KINGDOM

Some feathered friends offer Jada, Tim, and Cobble a ride. But beware—the clouds are not as fluffy as they first look.

Jump aboard a goldgull and steer it around the clouds.

Hold on tight, everyone!

CAN YOU FIND ...

4   5   6

To Gingerbread Town (page 18)

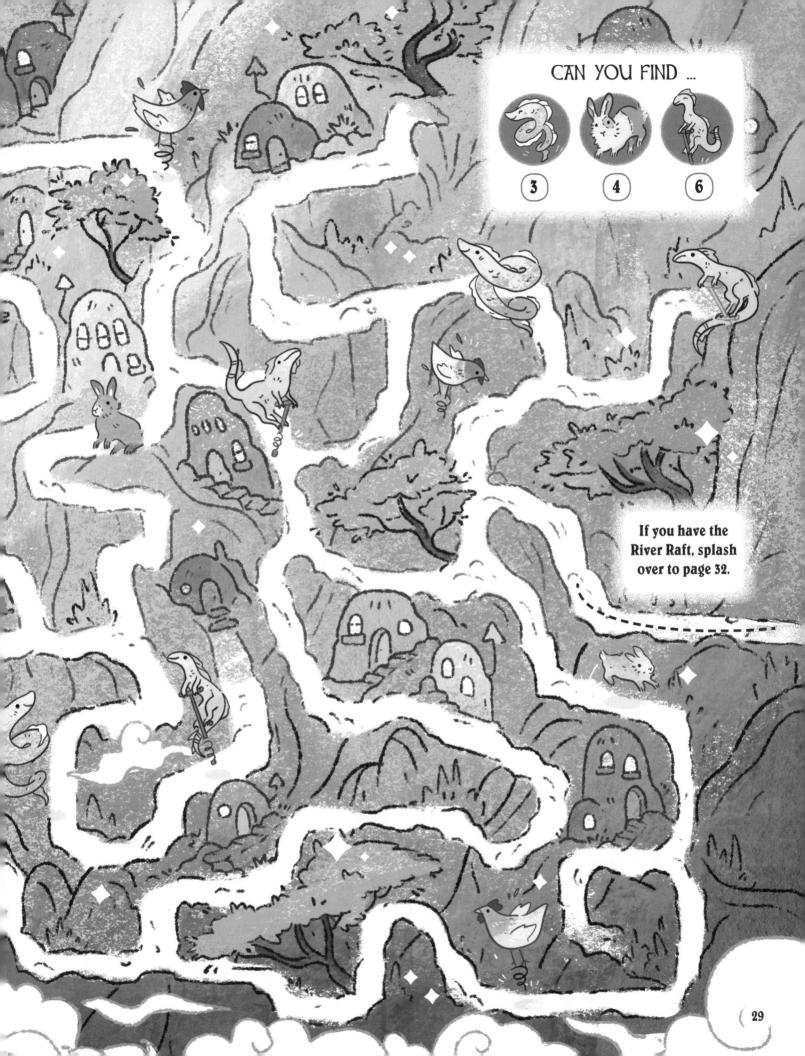

CAN YOU FIND ...

3 4 6

If you have the
River Raft, splash
over to page 32.

To Gingerbread Town (page 18)

Collect the River Raft.

To Bounceberg (page 28)

If you have the diving helmets, plunge to the Sunken City (page 36).

HUNGRY JUNGLE

The trio arrive in a wild jungle filled with sharp-toothed flowers. Can they get through without ending up as plant food? And look out—the Night Knight's back!

These plants are carnivorous. Try not to get added to the menu!

To the Sunken City (page 36)

To the Catacombs
(page 38)

Collect the Sea
Queen's Trident.

To the Hungry
Jungle (page 34)

CAN YOU FIND ...

3   4   5

To the Hungry
Jungle (page 34)

To the Sunken
City (page 36)

MOODY MOUNTAIN

The three heroes have a hard and slippery climb ahead, with the extra danger of ice traps and angry snowbeasts. Help them find a safe path!

If you have the River Raft, turn to page 42.

CAN YOU FIND ...

6 6 3

40

To the Thirsty Desert (page 44)

41

CAN YOU FIND ...

5   5   6

To the Crags
(page 52)

THIRSTY DESERT

The friends step onto golden sands. What a dry, arid place! Only the long-tongued aquadillos can sense the secret springs beneath the surface.

We'd better hurry through here or we'll pass out from thirst!

CAN YOU FIND ...

3   5   6

To the Dragon
Graveyard
(page 46)

To the Hungry
Jungle (page 34)

DRAGON GRAVEYARD

Next, the tired trio arrive at the graveyard of extinct battlebeasts. Is there a path through all the ancient bones?

Wow! These creatures must have been enormous!

CAN YOU FIND ...

2   4   5

BUBBLEBOROUGH

The three heroes find themselves in a floating garden populated by living balloon animals.

Step carefully here—you don't want to burst anyone!

Collect the Golden Gauntlet.

To the Dragon Graveyard (page 46)

CAN YOU FIND ...

1   1   1

To the Crags
(page 52)

To Bug Bridges
(page 50)

To the Shimmering
Streams (page 42)

To Bubbleborough
(page 48)

Collect the Winged Helmet

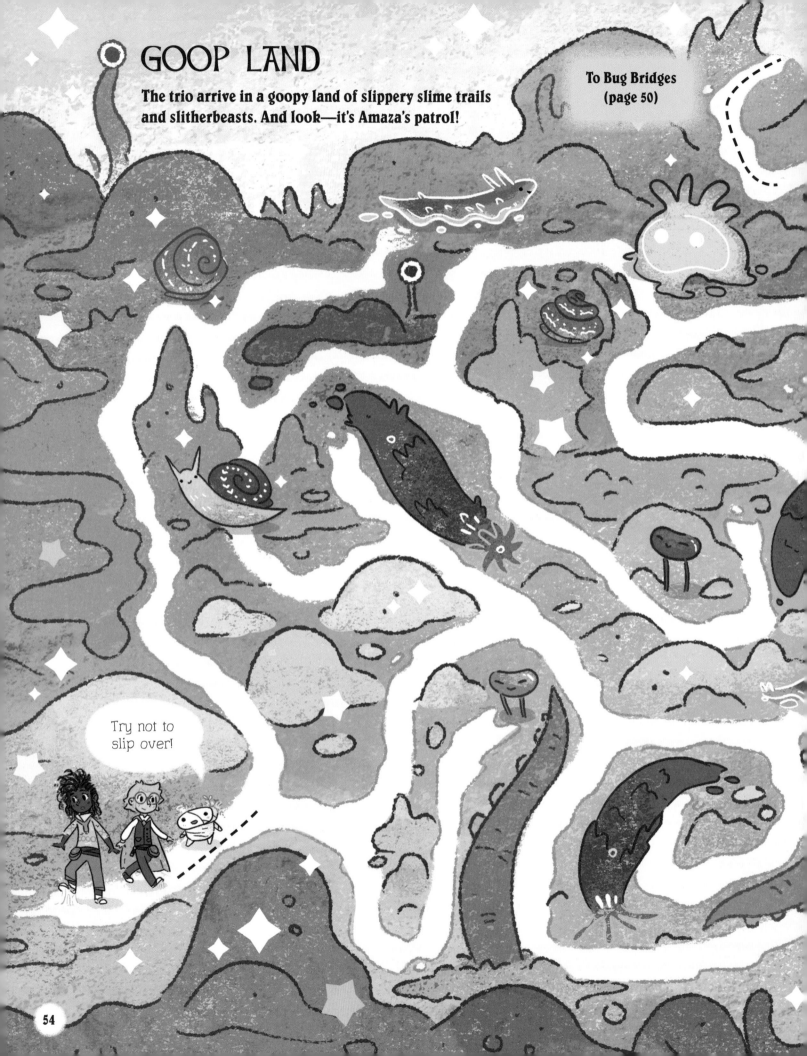

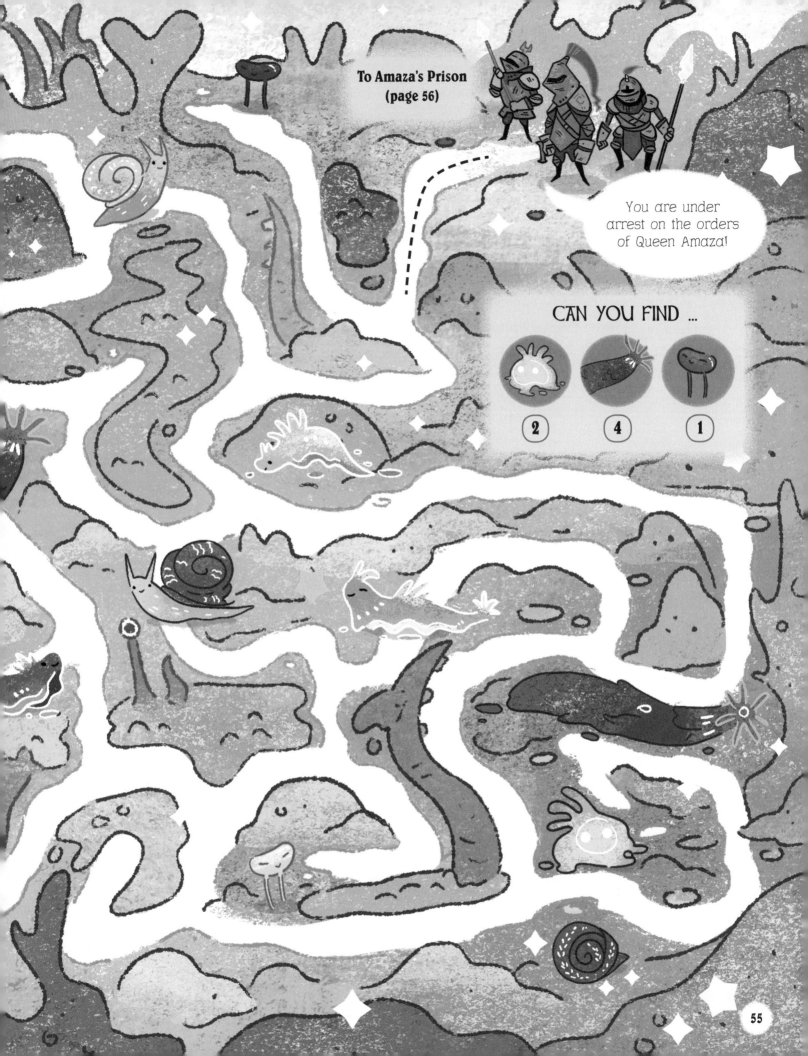

The guards took away your treasures. Collect them here!

To Amaza's Palace (Page 58)

CAN YOU FIND ...

4   6   7

To Goop Land (page 54)

ANSWERS

Key:

Maze route 1

Maze route 2

Search and find items

Treasure items to collect

Pages 4-5: Thornwood

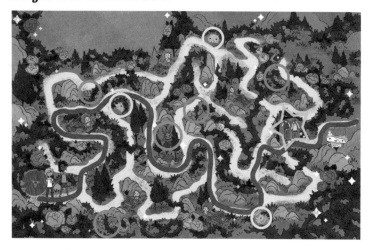

Pages 6-7: Shifting Swamp

Pages 8-9: Crystal Forest

Pages 10-11: Valley of Wisps

Pages 12-13: The Burrows

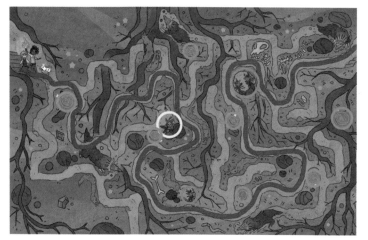

Pages 14-15: Lightning Land

Pages 16-17: Fire Fields

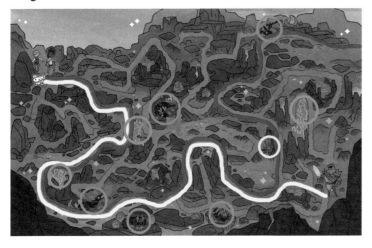

Pages 18-19: Gingerbread Town

Pages 20-21: Trappers' Glade

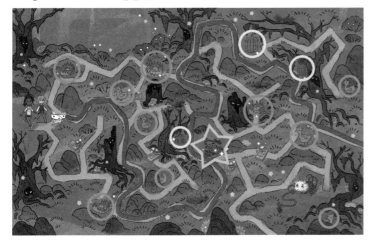

Pages 22-23: Tower Tree

Pages 24-25: The Eyrie

Pages 26-27: Sky Kingdom

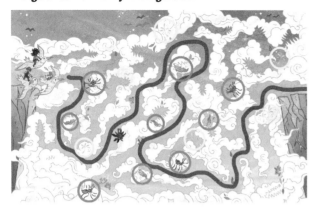

Pages 28-29: Bounceberg

Pages 30-31: Sparkling City

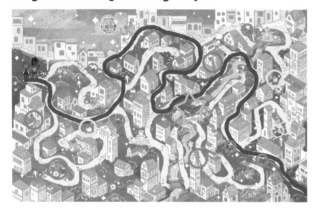

Pages 32-33: Cosmic Pool

Pages 34-35: Hungry Jungle

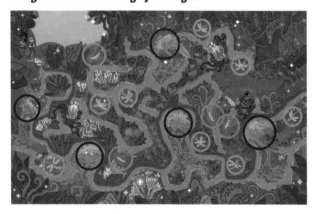

Pages 36-37: Sunken City

Pages 38-39: The Catacombs

Pages 40-41: Moody Mountain

Pages 42-43: Shimmering Streams

Pages 44-45: Thirsty Desert

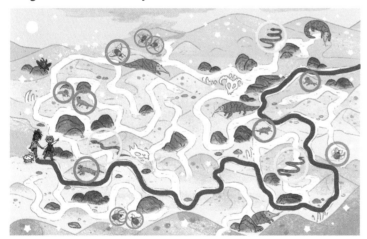

Pages 46-47: Dragon Graveyard

Pages 48-49: Bubbleborough

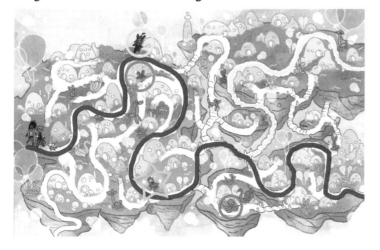

Pages 50-51: Bug Bridges

Pages 52-53: The Crags

Pages 54-55: Goop Land

Pages 56-57: Amaza's Prison

Pages 58-59: Amaza's Palace

ARCTURUS

This edition published in 2021 by Arcturus Publishing Limited
26/27 Bickels Yard, 151–153 Bermondsey Street,
London SE1 3HA

Author: William Potter
Illustrator: Laura Horton
Editor: Joe Harris
Designer: Sarah Fountain

ISBN: 978-1-3988-0738-9
CH008189NT
Supplier 29, Date 0521, Print run 9961

Printed in China

Page-by-Page Solution

**This is the quickest way for Jada and Tim to complete
their quest, but many other routes are possible.**

4–5 Thornwood (collect Quest Clothes) ➜ 6–7 Shifting
Swamp (collect Ancient Shield) ➜ 8–9 Crystal Forest
(collect Sun Gem) ➜ 10–11 Valley of Wisps (collect Eternal
Flame) ➜ 8–9 Crystal Forest again ➜ Use Eternal Flame
to access 12–13 The Burrows ➜ Use Sun Gem to access
16–17 Fire Fields ➜ 14–15 Lightning Land (collect Singing
Sword) ➜ 16–17 Fire Fields again ➜ Use Singing Sword
to access 20–21 Trappers' Glade (collect Climbing Gear)
➜ Use Climbing Gear to access 22–23 Tower Tree ➜
24–25 The Eyrie (collect Chainmail Shirt) ➜ 26–27 Sky
Kingdom ➜ 18–19 Gingerbread Town ➜ 30–31 Sparkling
City (collect River Raft) ➜ 28–29 Bounceberg ➜ Use
River Raft to access 32–33 Cosmic Pool (collect Diving
Helmets) ➜ Use Diving Helmets to access 36–37 Sunken
City (collect Sea Queen's Trident) ➜ 38–39 Catacombs
(collect Invisibility Cloak) ➜ 34–35 Hungry Jungle ➜
44–45 Thirsty Desert ➜ 46–47 Dragon Graveyard (collect
Eagle-Eye Bow) ➜ Back to 34–35 Hungry Jungle ➜ Use
Sea Queen's Trident to access 40–41 Moody Mountain
➜ Use River Raft to access 42–43 Shimmering Streams
➜ 52–53 The Crags (collect Winged Helmet) ➜ 48–49
Bubbleborough (collect Golden Gauntlet) ➜ 50–51 Bug
Bridges ➜ Use Invisibility Cloak to access 54–55 Goop
Land ➜ 56–57 Amaza's Prison ➜ 58–59 Amaza's Palace
➜ THE END